"How I Failed at Network Marketing to Succeed in Life"

By MJ MEREDITH

Copyright © 2025 by MJ Treloar
All rights reserved. No part of this publication may be reproduced, stored or transmitted in any form or by any means, electronic, mechanical, photocopying, recording, scanning, or otherwise without written permission from the publisher. It is illegal to copy this book, post it to a website, or distribute it by any other means without permission. MJ Treloar asserts the moral right to be identified as the author of this work.
First edition
ISBN 9781764201209 Print
9781764201216 Epub

- **Introduction: Welcome to My Failure 8**
  - Who Is This Book For? 9
  - Why Write a Book About Failure? 9
- **Chapter 1: Welcome to My Failure 14**
  - Chapter Summary: 16
  - Reflection Prompts: 17
  - Workbook Section: 18
  - Key Takeaway: 19
- **Chapter 2: The Dream They Sold Me 20**
  - The Honeymoon Phase 21
  - The First No 22
  - Chapter Summary: 24
  - Reflection Prompts: 25
  - Workbook Section: 26
  - Key Takeaway: 29
- **Chapter 3: Hustle Culture & False Starts 30**
  - The Burnout No One Talks About 31
  - Chapter 3 Summary: 33
  - Reflection Prompts: 34
  - Workbook Section: Breaking the Hustle Cycle .. 36
  - Key Takeaway: 39
- **Chapter 4: People Over Product 40**
  - When I Started Listening 41
  - What I Learned About People 42
  - I Came In to Sell. I Stayed to Connect 43
  - Chapter 4 Summary: 44
  - Reflection Prompts: 45
  - Workbook Section: 47
  - Key Takeaway: 49

Chapter 5: The Painful Lessons of Rejection..... 50
And Then It Got Worse... 51
Then Something Shifted... 52
What Rejection Taught Me About Life.................... 53
You Can't Avoid It—So Learn From It..................... 53
　Chapter 5 Summary:.. 55
　Reflection Prompts:.. 56
　Workbook Section:... 57
　Key Takeaway:... 59

Chapter 6: Discipline = Freedom......................... 60
The Unsexy Work That Changed Everything......... 61
The Hidden Freedom in Structure.......................... 63
So No, I Didn't Quit... 64
　Chapter 6 Summary... 65
　Reflection Prompts... 66
　Workbook Section.. 67
　Key Takeaway.. 69

Chapter 7: You Don't Need Permission.............. 70
The Power of Starting Before You're Ready.......... 71
This Was Never Just About Business..................... 72
　Chapter 7 Summary... 73
　Reflection Prompts:.. 74
　Workbook Section:... 76

Chapter 8: It Was Never About the Company..... 80
Leaving Without Bitterness..................................... 81
Redefining Success on My Terms.......................... 82
The Company Was Just the Start........................... 83
　Chapter 8 Summary:.. 84

- Reflection Prompts:... 85
- Workbook Section:... 87
- Key Takeaway:.. 89
- **Chapter 9: The Real Win — Who You Become... 90**
  - The Gap Between Who You Are and Who You Pretend to Be..90
  - I Didn't Win in the Way They Measured It..............91
  - You Don't Always Get What You Came For........... 92
  - Chapter 9 Summary:.. 93
  - Reflection Prompts:...94
  - Workbook Section:.. 96
  - Key Takeaway:.. 99
- **Chapter 10: How It All Shows Up Now............... 100**
  - The Transformation You Can't See......................100
  - The Company Was Never the Point..................... 101
  - You Didn't Fail. You Graduated............................101
  - How It Shows Up Now... 101
  - Chapter 10 Summary:.. 102
  - Reflection Prompts:... 103
  - Workbook Section:... 105
  - Key Takeaway:... 107
- **Epilogue: For the Ones Still in It........................108**
  - Recommended Reading List............................. 111

📖 Introduction: Welcome to My Failure

"So... how's that network thing of yours going?"

If you've ever been involved in network marketing — aka Multi-Level Marketing (MLM) — or honestly, *any* kind of hustle that sits outside the traditional 9-to-5, you've probably heard *that* question.

Probably with a smirk.

Probably from someone who already decided you were going to fail.

And maybe, eventually... you did, fail that is.

I did.

This isn't a rags-to-riches story. I'm not here to tell you how I climbed to the top of the leaderboard, won a car, or made six figures in six months.

Instead, this is the story of how I failed in network marketing — but learned skills, developed mindsets, and gained experiences that helped me succeed in life.

Most network marketing books tell you how to win. I'm here to share with you what to do when you don't.

Who Is This Book For?

This book is for:

- The ones who tried, gave it everything, and still walked away.

- The ones who felt like they weren't "cut out" for it.

- The ones who feel duped, burned out, or ashamed.

- And especially, the ones who are ready to own their failure and mine it for gold.

I want you to see what I see now: that trying — and "failing" — at network marketing might be the best thing that ever happened to you.

If you've ever asked, *"Was that all a waste of time and money?"* — I wrote this book for you.

Why Write a Book About Failure?

Because it wasn't really failure.

Sure, I didn't hit the rank. I didn't "retire my boss." I didn't build a team of thousands or earn residual income while sipping cocktails on a beach.

But what I **did** build was far more valuable:

- Resilience
- Emotional intelligence
- People skills
- Discipline
- Self-awareness
- And a completely different understanding of what success actually is.

Network marketing taught me to show up for myself, to face rejection, to speak to strangers — actually, something even more basic: how to communicate in general. It taught me to keep going when it was hard, to take radical ownership of my life, and to stop waiting for permission.

I didn't fail — I graduated.
 A graduate degree in failure — otherwise known as wisdom.

To me, **wisdom is simply failing enough to have learned.**

We're all so afraid of failure that most of us don't even try. We either do nothing, or we make some half-hearted attempt at chasing that dream.

But here's the truth:
The only difference between you and the person you think is successful is this — they did what you're still unwilling to do.

I know I'm being a little preachy here, but I've had so many conversations with incredible talented people who would be so much closer to their dream — or simply so much happier — if they were just willing to start. But fear (false evidence assumed real) or whatever story they're telling themselves holds them back. They don't even give themselves the chance.

I used to be called stubborn. I've since realised — I'm not stubborn. I'm steadfast.

There's a difference.
Stubborn says: "I won't."
Steadfast says: "I will."

And here's what I will do:

- I will work until the job is done.

- I will persevere until I make it.

- I will learn what I need to know.

- I will go where I need to go.

- I will keep going after I fail — until I learn.

- I will — until I succeed.

Failure isn't fatal. It's inevitable when you're pursuing something worthwhile.
 The real failure is never giving yourself the chance to begin.

So, was it really a failure?

Let's talk about what really matters.
 Let's look at what you truly gained.

Because you didn't fail.
 You learned.
 You grew.
 You became.

And that's success in its rawest form.

Welcome to the beginning of a different kind of story.

A Note About This Book:

Reading something inspirational is wonderful, but putting it into practice is where real change happens. To help you do just that, each chapter concludes with a:

- **Chapter Summary**

- **Reflection Prompts**

- **Workbook Section**

This book is designed to be practical, reflective, and meaningful — so you can walk away with more than just good intentions.

Let's get started.

📖Chapter 1: Welcome to My Failure

"So… how's that little business of yours going?"

If I had a dollar for every time someone asked me that—half-joking, half-skeptical—I probably would've made more than I did in network marketing.

When I first joined, I was *all in*.
 Fired up. Ready to break free from the 9-to-5 grind, claim my "time freedom," and build a life on my own terms. I listened to the audios, showed up to the Zoom calls, read the books they told us to read, and practiced my pitch in the mirror like I was preparing for *Shark Tank*.

I wanted it—badly.
 I believed in the product.
 I believed in the system.
 I believed in myself.

And then… it didn't work.
 Or more accurately, **it didn't work the way I thought it would.**

My friends stopped replying.
 My social media posts got quiet likes, but no comments.
 I spent more money on products and training than I ever made in commissions.

I tried to keep the energy up—to *fake it 'til I made it*—but inside, I felt like a fraud. Embarrassed. Tired. Like maybe I just wasn't cut out for it.

Eventually, I quit.

I told people I was "stepping away to focus on other things," but really? I was just exhausted. Tired of trying so hard to make something work that clearly wasn't meant for me.

At the time, it felt like failure.
 A big, public, soul-crushing failure.

I had to swallow my pride and walk away from something I'd shouted about from the rooftops just months before.

But here's the twist:
 That so-called failure changed my life.

When the dust settled, I realised something... I was different. Stronger. More grounded. More aware of who I was—and who I wasn't.

Network marketing didn't make me rich.
 But it did teach me how to talk to people.
 It taught me how to handle rejection and be resilient.
 How to be consistent.
 How to show up, even when no one was watching.
 How to set goals, chase them, and learn from the crash landing if I didn't make it.

Most of all, it taught me that **discipline is freedom**—and that failure isn't fatal, nor is it the opposite of success. **It's the fuel for it.**

This book is the story of how I failed in network marketing… and somehow ended up with everything I actually needed.

If you've tried and "failed" at it too, you're not alone.

This book is for you.

Let's dive in.

Chapter Summary:

In this chapter, I share the honest story of stepping into network marketing with high hopes and determination, only to find that my path didn't lead where I thought it would. What seemed like failure at the time became one of the most transformative experiences of my life. I walked away not with the financial freedom I expected, but with life-changing skills: resilience, discipline, communication, and a new understanding of success.
This chapter sets the tone for reframing failure—not as defeat, but as a launchpad for growth.

🖊 Reflection Prompts:

- When have you gone *"all in"* on something that didn't turn out the way you hoped?

- How did you feel about yourself in that moment? Ashamed, frustrated, confused? Be honest.

- Can you now identify skills or lessons you walked away with—even if you didn't realise it at the time?

- How do you currently define failure? Has that definition helped you—or held you back?

- If you were to tell your own *"failure"* story, what would the opening sentence be?

📔 Workbook Section:

✏️ Exercise 1: Rewriting Your Failure Narrative

Think about a time you feel you *"failed."* In the space below, briefly describe the situation.

- What did you originally think you lost?

- What unexpected skills, strengths, or self-awareness did you gain from the experience?

- If you were to retell this story as a success disguised as failure, what would the new headline be?

Example:
Old Headline: "I failed at running a business."
New Headline: "I discovered what really drives me and developed unstoppable resilience."

Exercise 2: Define Success (Your Way)

- Write your personal definition of success.

- What does success look like to you now?

- How is that different from the version you chased before?

Key Takeaway:

Failure isn't the end. It's often the best beginning.

📖 Chapter 2: The Dream They Sold Me

They told me I could be free.

They told me I could fire my boss, work from anywhere, and earn more in a month than most people make in a year.

I didn't need a business degree. I didn't need inventory. I didn't need to be special—just "coachable" and "hungry."

At the time, I was both.

I wasn't miserable, but I wasn't lit up by my life either. I was working, paying bills, doing what I was supposed to do—but I wanted more. More freedom, more fulfillment, more income. More purpose.

So when someone I trusted told me they had an *"opportunity,"* I said YES—without really knowing what I was saying yes to.

It sounded perfect.
 Work on your own terms.
 Be your own boss.
 Live life "by design."

And maybe that's what I wanted most: to be in charge of me.

So I signed up. Bought the starter kit. Watched the welcome video. Got added to the Facebook group filled with "rockstars." Everyone was smiling, excited, and living their best lives.

I was so sure I was on the brink of something big.

The Honeymoon Phase

The first few months were electric.

I started talking differently—about growth, mindset, goals. I was up early, reading books I'd never touched before (it was the first time in my life I'd actually read a book cover to cover). I felt productive. Inspired. Important.

I had a purpose. A mission. A team.

And for the first time in a long time... I was dreaming again.

I made a vision board. I wrote down my *"WHY."* I pictured the day I'd hand my boss my resignation letter and never look back. I pictured the car, the house, the holidays and overseas trips.

I imagined people clapping for me at a huge event while I crossed a stage in heels and some designer outfit I couldn't yet afford.

It was intoxicating.

And honestly, that's part of the magic.
 Network marketing gives you permission to dream out loud.
 To want more—unapologetically.

But what they don't always prepare you for... is the cost of the dream.

The First No

It happened fast.

I sent my first message to someone I knew—confident they'd be excited. I mean, why wouldn't they be? This was an amazing opportunity!

They left me on **read**.

The second one said, *"Is this one of those illegal pyramid things?"*

The third one laughed and said, *"Good luck with that."*

It stung. Not just because I was trying to build a business—but because it made me question myself.

Was I being naive?
 Was I annoying people?
 Was I just chasing a fantasy?

Suddenly, the motivational quotes started to feel thin.
The *"just keep pushing!"* advice didn't hit the same.

But I wasn't ready to give up. Not yet.

So I pushed harder.

I wrote the posts. I followed the scripts. I tried to "add value." I copied what the top leaders were doing. I sent cold messages, showed up to every training session, and told myself that if I just worked harder—it would work.

But inside, something started to shift.

I wasn't just selling a product or a service.

I was selling a dream.
 One I wasn't sure I believed in anymore.

And that's when I learned something no one told me at the start:

In this business, your biggest sale… is to yourself.

Every. Single. Day.

You sell yourself the belief that this will work.
 That you're on the right path.
 That your breakthrough is just one more call, one more post, one more *yes* away.

And maybe it is.

But what happens when the *yes* doesn't come?
What happens when belief turns into burnout?

That's where we'll go next.

 Chapter Summary:

In this chapter, I unpack the intoxicating promise of network marketing—the dream of freedom, wealth, purpose, and self-determination. I share the excitement of the "honeymoon phase," where growth feels electric, the future feels limitless, and the dream seems within reach. But I also reveal the emotional cost: the sting of rejection, the internal doubt, and the moment when you realise you're not just selling a product—you're selling belief, especially to yourself. The real work isn't just convincing others. It's convincing yourself to keep going, even when the cracks start to show.

✒ Reflection Prompts:

- What was the dream that first pulled you into your network marketing or personal growth journey? Can you describe it vividly?

- Did you ever get caught up in the energy of the community or the promise of success? What did that feel like for you?

- When did you start feeling the first signs of doubt or disillusionment? Was there a specific conversation, rejection, or moment that stuck with you?

- Do you still believe in parts of the dream? Which parts feel real to you now, and which parts feel like someone else's script?

- How often do you find yourself "selling" belief to yourself in other areas of life? Is that empowering or exhausting?

Workbook Section:

Exercise 1: The Honeymoon Reflection

Write about the first 2-3 weeks of your network marketing journey—or a time when you were fully swept up in a new dream.

- What were you excited about?

- What did your days look like?

- What books, people, or messages inspired you?

- How did you feel when you woke up in the morning?

Exercise 2: The Cost of the Dream

List what you invested (emotionally, financially, socially) in the pursuit of this dream.

Examples:

- Time spent away from family and friends | Money spent on products or trainings | Emotional energy spent overcoming rejection | Friendships that became strained

Was the dream worth the cost? Why or why not?

✏️ Exercise 3: Your Dream, Reimagined

If you could design your own version of the dream—without the scripts, pressure, or someone else's timeline—what would it look like?

- What would freedom feel like to you now?

- What kind of work would make you feel alive?

- How would you define success on your terms?

Write your reimagined dream in the space below as if it's already real.

Example:
"I wake up each day knowing I'm building a life of creativity, connection, and steady progress. I define success by joy, not just income. I choose meaningful work, and I give myself permission to pivot without guilt."

◎ Key Takeaway:

It's okay to dream. It's powerful to dream on your own terms.

📖 Chapter 3: Hustle Culture & False Starts

I thought I had a work ethic — until I joined the team group chat.

Every morning, I'd see posts from people celebrating their 4:30am "power hour," showing screenshots of 25 cold messages sent before sunrise. They'd say things like, *"No excuses, just results,"* or, *"Your dreams don't care how tired you are."*

And for a while, I bought into it.

Because if I wasn't succeeding yet, it must be because I wasn't working hard enough, right?

So I pushed. I turned my free time into work time. Lunchtime at my job became time for follow-ups. Nights were spent on Zoom calls. Weekends were for training sessions and three-way calls and trying to get people to *"just take a look at this."*

My phone might as well have been another limb—I couldn't put it down. I was always "on."

The more I hustled, the more I convinced myself that a breakthrough was just around the corner. After all, that's what the leaders always said:

"You're one message away from a life-changing conversation."
 "The only difference between you and the top earners is consistency."
 "Do what others won't for a few years so you can live how others can't for the rest of your life."

So I sacrificed. Sleep, rest, social time. I started saying things like, *"I can't, I've got a call,"* more than I care to admit.

It felt like I was moving forward.
 It felt like momentum.

But I wasn't actually getting results.
 I was just getting busier.

The Burnout No One Talks About

Hustle feels good — until it doesn't.

After an extended period (longer than I would have liked to admit to myself) of going all-in, I hit a wall.

I was exhausted, discouraged, and quietly resentful. My results weren't matching my effort, and it started to mess with my head.

Maybe I'm not cut out for this.
 Maybe I'm lazy.
 Maybe success just isn't in the cards for me.

It wasn't just physical burnout — it was emotional, mental, and spiritual. I was pouring so much energy into something with no return, and worst of all, I felt like I couldn't tell anyone.

Because in hustle culture, complaining can be perceived as a weakness.
 And quitting? That's failure.

So I stayed silent and kept pretending.

Kept posting. Kept smiling. Kept showing up to the team calls and clapping for other people's wins while wondering if I'd ever have my own.

Outside the business, I was drifting. I missed family gatherings because I was *"just quickly jumping on a call."* I stopped doing the things I loved, like reading or walking without a phone in my hand. Even when I was physically present, my mind was somewhere else — always chasing the next conversation, the next goal, the next win that never seemed to arrive.

This is what no one talks about in the highlight reels:
 → The part where your effort doesn't equal your outcome.
 → The part where you lose more belief in yourself with each rejection.
 → The part where more hustle just digs the hole deeper.

Eventually, I learned the difference between activity and productivity.
 I learned that not all movement is progress.

And most importantly, I learned that chasing someone else's version of success will always leave you feeling behind.

It took stepping away from the noise to hear my own voice again.
 But that came later.

First, I had to stop trying to be the perfect rep... and start remembering who I actually was.

That was the beginning of something I hadn't expected — I was about to unlearn everything hustle culture had taught me. And I didn't know it yet, but that would change everything.

Chapter 3 Summary:

This chapter explores how hustle culture in network marketing can become a toxic treadmill—one where more effort doesn't always mean more success. I share how I bought into the "no excuses" mindset, sacrificed rest and personal time, and kept pushing in the hope of a breakthrough that never came. The more I hustled, the more I lost touch with myself, chasing activity over actual progress. I reflect on the emotional burnout that creeps in when effort isn't rewarded, the quiet toll it takes on your life outside the business, and how learning to separate productivity from busywork eventually helped me step off the hustle wheel.

✏️ Reflection Prompts:

- Have you ever mistaken busyness for progress? What did that look like in your life?

- How did hustle culture affect your relationships, health, or self-perception?

- What story were you telling yourself about success? Was it *"I must work harder"* or *"I'm not doing enough"*?

- When was the last time you celebrated rest as an achievement?

- If you could rebuild your daily rhythm, what would balance look like for you now?

📓 Workbook Section: Breaking the Hustle Cycle

Exercise 1: Activity vs. Productivity Audit

Create two columns:
 Column 1: Activities you regularly did in your network marketing hustle.
 Column 2: Results directly tied to those activities (income, growth, meaningful conversations).

Activities	Results

Look at your list:

- Which activities made you feel busy but didn't create results? (you could simply put a red X beside the activity)

- Which activities genuinely moved you closer to your goals? (put a big tick beside the activity)

- What could you have done less of? What should you have done more of? (use an arrow down for less and an arrow up for more)

Exercise 2: Rest Inventory

List five things you used to enjoy before you got caught in the hustle cycle.

1.
2.
3.
4.
5.

Example:

- Reading for pleasure | Long walks without my phone | Cooking without multitasking | Spending time with family without thinking about work | Creative hobbies

How can you intentionally reintegrate one or more of these into your life now?

Exercise 3: Redefining Success

Write your new success statement:
"Success for me now looks like ……."

Example:
"Success for me now looks like meaningful work that fits into a balanced life where I can rest, grow, and connect."

How does this new version of success feel compared to the hustle-driven one?

◎ Key Takeaway:

True progress isn't about doing more—it's about doing what matters. Rest isn't a reward; it's a requirement.

📖 Chapter 4: People Over Product

At first, I thought I was selling a product.

That's what I signed up for, right? A great product, a compensation plan, a system. I thought if I learned the features, memorized the benefits, and nailed the pitch, I'd be set.

So I got to work — ticking the boxes, following the formula.

Send the message ✅
Book the call ✅
Deliver the script ✅
Follow up in two days ✅

But pretty quickly, I noticed something strange…

The more I pushed the product, the more people pulled away.

It wasn't about the ingredients.
It wasn't about the "life-changing opportunity."
It wasn't even about the price.

It was about me.

I was so focused on getting the "yes" that I forgot I was talking to actual human beings — with real lives, real hesitations, and real feelings.

I had been trained to believe that objections were just excuses to be "overcome." That a "no" really meant "not yet." That if someone didn't buy in, they just didn't see the value.

But eventually, I realized something important:

People don't buy products. People buy trust.

When I Started Listening

One day, I stopped following the script.

A friend I hadn't spoken to in a while messaged me to "catch up," and instead of turning the conversation into a pitch like I was taught… I just talked to her.

We chatted about life, relationships, work stress — everything but the business.

At the end of the conversation, she said, "Actually, I've been meaning to ask about that product you're using — I think I might want to give it a try."

And that's when it clicked.

The product didn't open the door. The connection did.

The more I thought about it, the more I realized how awkward and transactional I had been. Honestly? It stung. I felt embarrassed when I looked back at all the conversations I'd bulldozed in the name of chasing a sale.

From that point on, I changed my approach. I focused less on selling and more on serving. Less on getting people into something, and more on understanding where they were already at.

I asked more questions. I listened better. I stopped interrupting people's stories in my head with thoughts like, How can I close this?

And ironically, the less I tried to "convert" people, the more open they became.

What I Learned About People

Network marketing gave me a crash course in human nature. It taught me things I never learned in school — like:

- *How to actually listen, without just waiting for my turn to speak*

- *How to read tone, body language, hesitation*

- *How to handle awkward conversations with grace*

- *How to stop taking rejection personally*

- *How to ask better questions*

- *How to care — even when there's no sale on the line*

I remember one woman whose silence on a call told me more than her words did. Another friend was hesitant, not because of the price, but because she didn't believe she could succeed. I started noticing these moments — things I would've bulldozed right over when I was busy trying to "get the close."

These are skills I still use every single day.

Not in a sales funnel. Not on a call. But in real life — with my friends, my clients, my coworkers, my family, even strangers.

I Came In to Sell. I Stayed to Connect.

Ironically, the moment I stopped trying to be a salesperson… I started becoming a better human.

Network marketing didn't make me rich, but it made me real. It stripped away a lot of my people-pleasing and attempted perfectionism. It taught me to see people, not just "target" them.

If you've been in the game, you know this truth already:

The real product is you.
And people can feel when you're only there to get something from them.

Once I stopped seeing everyone as a potential "prospect," life got a lot lighter. And ironically, that's when the real opportunities started showing up — the kind I didn't have to chase.

> *"People may forget what you said, they may forget what you did, but they will never forget how you made them feel." — Maya Angelou*

When I stopped chasing people, I started finding the right ones.
And that's when things really started to shift.

 ## *Chapter 4 Summary:*

In this chapter, I share a critical turning point: the realization that success in network marketing isn't about

pushing products—it's about genuinely connecting with people. I started out believing that scripts and checklists would create success, but I soon noticed the harder I sold, the more people pulled away. The breakthrough came when I abandoned the pitch and simply focused on building real, human connections. Trust became the key—not the product. The chapter emphasizes that people buy from those they know, like, and trust—and that authenticity, curiosity, and care create far more meaningful opportunities than aggressive sales tactics ever could. I learned that the most valuable skills were listening, caring, and building trust—lessons I still use every day.

✏ *Reflection Prompts:*

- *When was the last time you felt truly heard by someone? How did that experience make you feel?*

- *Can you think of a time when you were more focused on "getting the sale" than truly understanding the person you were talking to? How did that conversation go?*

- *What would change if you approached your next conversation with genuine curiosity, with no agenda?*

- *What does "serving over selling" mean to you? How can you embody this in your current life or work?*

- *Are there people in your life you've been "prospecting" instead of simply connecting with? What might happen if you let go of the outcome?*

Workbook Section:

Exercise 1: Connection Check-In

List three people you've recently spoken to (in business or in life). For each, answer:

	Did I truly listen, or was I thinking about what to say next?	*Did I ask questions that showed real interest?*	*Did I make them feel seen, valued, or heard?*
Person 1			
Person 2			
Person 3			

Exercise 2: Build Conversations, Not Pitches

Write out three questions you can use in future conversations that:

- *Have nothing to do with sales, products, or business*

- *Are genuinely curious about the person's life, passions, or challenges*

Question 1:

Question 2:

Question 3:

Example:

- "What's lighting you up right now?"
- "What's been the best part of your week so far?"
- "If you could create your ideal day, what would it look like?"

Exercise 3: Serving Over Selling

Think about your current work, hobby, or personal goals. List three ways you can serve people today without expecting anything in return.

Way 1:

Way 2:

Way 3:

Example:

- *Send someone an encouraging message.*
- *Share a helpful article without a sales link.*
- *Introduce two people who might support each other.*

◎ **Key Takeaway:**

When you shift from "What can I get?" to "How can I serve?", trust naturally follows—and trust is the foundation of all meaningful success.

📖 Chapter 5: The Painful Lessons of Rejection

Alongside network marketing, I've also worked in call centres — both inbound and outbound — where rejection is part of the daily script. And I'll admit, I used to take it very personally.

Harder than I care to admit.

Every abusive hang-up.
Every ignored message.
Every polite brush-off.
Every friend who stopped liking my posts or suddenly got "too busy to catch up."

Each one stung—not just because I didn't get the sale or the sign-up, but because it felt like they were rejecting me.

And that's the problem with network marketing when you're new:
You're taught to be the brand.
To make your business part of your identity.
To show up "authentically"—but only if that authenticity is positive, upbeat, and inspirational.

So when someone says no to the product… it feels like they're saying no to you.
 When someone unfollows your journey… it feels like they're unfollowing you.

And for a while, that pain stopped me from showing up fully.
 I hesitated before posting.
 Second-guessed myself before reaching out.
 Feared the silence that came after "Hey! I think you'd be amazing at what I'm doing ✦✦ "

It was exhausting.

And Then It Got Worse

There was one week I'll never forget. I set myself a goal to send out a ridiculous amount of messages. Real, intentional ones. I crafted every message carefully. Personalised them. Tried to make each one feel natural.

Out of 50 people, only 3 replied.

One said no.
 One ghosted after the second message.
 One said, *"Please don't message me about stuff like this again."*

That was the day I almost quit.

I sat there, staring at my phone, wondering if I was just wasting my time. I'd followed all the advice, done all the right things, and all I had to show for it was silence.

Because rejection isn't just a moment in this business—it can feel like a lifestyle.

Then Something Shifted

The top earners always said things like:
"Every no gets you closer to a yes."

At first, it sounded like just another motivational quote.
But over time, I realised: rejection is the cost of showing up.
It's not a sign that you're failing—it's a sign that you're in the game.

The people who never hear "no" are the ones who never ask.

So I started celebrating the rejections.
I reframed the silence.
Every ignored message meant I was putting myself out there.
Every awkward conversation meant I was growing thicker skin.
Every *"I'm not interested"* became a tiny badge of courage I could pin to my sleeve.

And slowly... it stopped hurting.

Not because I stopped caring—but because I stopped depending on people's approval to feel worthy.

What Rejection Taught Me About Life

The gift of rejection didn't just apply to network marketing. It showed up in my relationships, my work life, and even my self-talk.

I started asking for what I wanted more confidently—even outside the business.
 I stopped filtering myself just to keep other people comfortable.
 I became more resilient. More assertive. More real.

Because when you stop fearing rejection, you start moving forward with power.
 You stop waiting for permission.
 You stop negotiating with your dreams.
 You stop settling for safety over authenticity.

And that's when things get interesting.

You Can't Avoid It—So Learn From It

There's no version of success—in business or in life—that doesn't involve hearing the word no.

I'm going to repeat that, because some of you need to see it or hear it twice:

There's no version of success—in business or in life—that doesn't involve hearing the word no.

You can either hide from it, or grow through it.

Network marketing gave me a PhD in rejection—and I'm thankful for every lesson. Because it taught me something school never did:
Rejection is not about you.
It's about fit, timing, readiness, belief.

And sometimes, people say no because they're scared—not because you're wrong.

So let them say no.
Let them roll their eyes.
Let them talk.

You're not here for everyone.

Some will, some won't, so what, next.

This is a mantra I heard from a brilliant leader—apologies, I can't remember who or even if they were the first to share these words of wisdom. It's not a statement meant to be disrespectful or dismissive—it's a reminder not to attach our emotions to the no's.

It's a reminder that you're here for growth.
And growth starts right on the other side of "no."

Because when you stop fearing rejection, you start chasing what really matters—and that's where the story goes next.

Chapter 5 Summary:

In this chapter, I open up about one of the hardest parts of network marketing: rejection. From ignored messages and abrupt hang-ups to friends who distanced themselves, the sting of "no" felt deeply personal—especially when being part of the brand meant tying my identity to the business. It's easy to feel that people aren't just rejecting the offer, but rejecting you. That mindset can silence you, make you hesitate, and eventually wear you down.

But something shifted: rejection became proof of action. It became a sign of courage, a step closer to growth, and ultimately, an essential part of the journey. I reframed rejection as necessary, not as something to avoid. This realisation didn't just transform my business—it changed how I lived. I became more assertive, resilient, and authentic across all areas of life.

The message is clear: rejection isn't the enemy. It's the gateway to growth, and avoiding it means missing the lessons that come from showing up. The mantra that carries this chapter is: **"Some will, some won't, so what, next."**

✏ Reflection Prompts:

- Think about a time when you took rejection personally. What story did you tell yourself at that moment?

- How do you typically react to rejection—do you retreat, push harder, or shut down? Why?

- What would it look like if you saw rejection as a badge of courage rather than a failure?

- Where in your life are you avoiding asking for what you truly want because you fear hearing "no"?

- How can you practice detaching your self-worth from other people's responses?

Workbook Section:

Exercise 1: Rejection Reframe Log

Over the next 7 days, track moments when you feel rejected (in any area of life). For each one, answer:

- What happened?

- How did I initially feel?

    What's a new way I can interpret this situation (what else could this mean)?

- What action can I take next that honours my growth instead of my fear?

Example:
Rejection: A friend didn't respond to my invite.
Initial feeling: Embarrassed and hurt.
Reframe: Maybe they're just busy. This isn't about me.
Next step: Keep inviting people without fear of silence.

Exercise 2: The Courage Counter

Set a goal to collect "no's" instead of "yes's" this week.

Write down:
My goal: I will collect ___ no's this week.
(**Example**: *I will collect 10 no's.*)

Each time you hear no, check it off as a win:
- ☐ No 1
- ☐ No 2
- ☐ No 3
...

When you reach your goal, reflect:

- How did it feel to actively pursue rejection?

- Did the sting of "no" soften over time?

- What did you learn about yourself?

Exercise 3: The Permission Slip

Write yourself a permission slip:

PERMISSION SLIP
I hereby give MYSELF permission to:

Signed:..
The Authoritative Party

Example:

I give myself permission to:

- Ask boldly
- Show up imperfectly
- Be seen
- Keep going after no
- Grow without everyone's approval

Write it, sign it, and keep it somewhere visible.

◎ Key Takeaway:

You don't grow by chasing only yes. You grow by showing up, hearing no, and moving forward anyway.

📖 Chapter 6: Discipline = Freedom

One unexpected thing network marketing taught me?

How to get out of my own way.

Before I got into the industry, I thought I was at least a little disciplined.
 I worked hard. I showed up. I got things done… eventually.
 But the truth?

I only really moved when I *felt* like it.
 If motivation didn't show up, neither did I.

Then network marketing came along and basically said:
"Cool story. Do it anyway."

The top leaders didn't wait for a mood.
 They didn't care if it was raining, if they were tired, or if they'd had a rough day.
 They showed up — daily, consistently, with intention.

And for the first time, I had no choice but to build real structure in my life.

There were:

- Calls to join
- Messages to send
- Books to read
- Trainings to attend
- Content to post
- And growth work to do

At first, it felt like a lot.
But over time... it gave me something I didn't even know I was missing:

Rhythm. Accountability. Ownership.

The Unsexy Work That Changed Everything

We live in a world obsessed with hacks, shortcuts, and "life-changing" routines.
But network marketing quietly taught me something deeper:
What you do daily determines where you end up.

It wasn't the big, flashy moments that changed me. It was the repetition:

- Reading a few pages of a book every day
- Posting consistently, even when no one engaged
- Setting small goals — and actually tracking them
- Choosing discomfort on purpose — not once, but daily

It wasn't sexy.
It wasn't glamorous.
It was often invisible.

But slowly... those habits started shifting my identity.
I stopped seeing myself as someone who *tries*.
I started seeing myself as someone who *executes*.

Discipline wasn't about restriction.
It was about reclaiming my power.

Because once I stopped outsourcing my progress to how I *felt*, I started moving — regardless of whether it was convenient or not.

And *that*, ironically, is what created the freedom I'd been chasing all along.

The Hidden Freedom in Structure

We're taught that freedom means doing what you want, when you want.
But if that's all you do, you end up a slave to your impulses.

You spin in cycles.
You procrastinate.
You crash and restart — over and over.

Real freedom?
It's being in control of your time, your energy, your choices.
It's waking up with clarity instead of chaos.
It's finishing the day proud of what you created — not guilty about what you didn't do.

And weirdly enough, I have a multi-level marketing company to thank for that.

No, I didn't hit the top rank.
No, I didn't walk the stage or drive the car.

But I did build something far more powerful:

Self-respect.

Because once you learn how to be disciplined — especially when no one's watching — you become unstoppable.

Career.
Relationships.
Creativity.
Even health.
(Though let's be honest — I'm still a work in progress there. Yes, I sometimes eat ice cream for dinner. It's called balance.)

It all grows from the same root:
Daily effort, multiplied over time.

So No, I Didn't Quit

People sometimes ask me:
"So did you quit the business?"

And my answer is always this:
I didn't quit. I graduated.

I kept the tools that served me — the habits, the mindset, the rhythm — and left the hype behind.

The product may not be in my life anymore.
But the structure? The personal growth? The discipline?

They're permanent.

And if nothing else, I'll always be grateful for that.
Because discipline became the foundation for everything else I've built since.

Chapter 6 Summary

In this chapter, we explore the unexpected but life-changing lesson from network marketing:
Discipline isn't restriction — it's liberation.

Before joining the industry, I worked when I "felt like it," stuck in cycles of motivation and burnout.
 But network marketing demanded consistency, structure, and commitment — not just when it was convenient.

The boring, invisible habits (sending messages, reading, showing up daily) built rhythm.
 That rhythm transformed my identity — from someone who dabbled... to someone who delivered.

The discipline I learned gave me back control — over my time, my energy, and ultimately, my freedom.

I didn't quit. I graduated.

Reflection Prompts

- Where in your life are you still waiting to "feel like it" before taking action?

- What small, daily habit could build momentum toward a goal you've been avoiding?

- How do you currently define freedom? Is it serving you — or keeping you stuck?

- What would it look like to take full responsibility for your growth, even when no one's watching?

- Where can you apply more consistency, even if it's not immediately rewarding?

Workbook Section

Exercise 1: Feelings vs. Action Tracker

In your diary or journal, for the next 5 days, track:

- Did I feel like doing the task? Yes / No

- Did I do it anyway? Yes / No

At the end of each day, reflect:

- How often did I rely on motivation?

- How often did I move without it?

- What changed in how I see myself?

Example:

☐ Follow-up messages
→ Did I feel like it? No → Did I do it anyway? Yes

☐ 10-minute walk
→ Did I feel like it? Yes → Did I do it anyway? Yes

☐ Write content
→ Did I feel like it? No → Did I do it anyway? No

Exercise 2: The Micro-Habit Builder (KaiZen)

Choose one small habit that will move you forward (should take less than 5 minutes a day):

Examples:

- Write 2 sentences for a future post
- Read 2 pages of a book
- Send 1 intentional message

Write yours below:

My micro-habit:

_____

I will do this every day for: ____ days

I will track it using: (calendar, journal, checklist)

Repetition creates rhythm. Rhythm creates results.

Exercise 3: Freedom Redefined

Complete this sentence:

> "I used to think freedom meant
> ……………………………………………………,
>
> but now I know freedom is
> ……………………………………………….."

Example:

> *"I used to think freedom meant doing nothing on hard days, but now I know freedom is doing what matters — even on hard days."*

Now list 3 areas in your life where you'll practise this new definition:

1.

2.

3.

🎯 Key Takeaway

Discipline isn't punishment — it's the path to self-respect, confidence, and true freedom.

📖 Chapter 7: You Don't Need Permission

One of the most unexpected gifts network marketing gave me? Audacity.
Not arrogance. Not overconfidence.
But a quiet, steadfast belief that whispers:
"I don't need to be chosen. I don't need anyone else's permission. I'll go first anyway."

Before this journey began, I was the type who needed to be invited.
To be told I was ready.
To wait until I felt qualified before I started anything.

> *(Reflective note: Network marketing was my first invitation to a future different from the everyday.)*

I thought success came to people who got picked —
The right résumé. The right degree. The right background.
People who had authority.

And then network marketing said:
"Here's your login. You're in business."
No gatekeeper.
No interview.
No one asking for credentials.
Just… go.

It felt crazy at first.
Who was I to start a business?
To post like a leader when I barely believed in myself?
To talk about personal development when I was still deeply under construction?

But the wildest part? **No one stopped me.**
Most people are too wrapped up in their own lives to notice whether you feel ready or not.

And in that space, something shifted:
I gave myself permission to act like the person I was becoming.

The Power of Starting Before You're Ready

If you wait until you feel ready, you'll never start.
Network marketing shoved me into motion.
It said, "Figure it out as you go."

And the truth is — that's how everything works.

Want to be a speaker? Start speaking.
Want to be a leader? Start leading.
Want to grow? Put yourself in rooms where you feel behind — and stay long enough to catch up.

It's never been about waiting for the right opportunity.
It's about becoming the kind of person who can create one.

That shift — from reacting to initiating — is one of the biggest things I carried with me out of the business and into the rest of my life.

I stopped asking:
"Is this okay?"
"Am I allowed?"
"Who am I to do this?"

And started asking:
"Why not me?"
"What if I just tried?"
"What's the worst that happens — I grow?"

This Was Never Just About Business

The biggest breakthrough wasn't financial.
It was internal.

I stopped waiting to be picked.
I stopped shrinking to fit into other people's expectations.
I stopped outsourcing my confidence to someone else's opinion.

That boldness started to show up everywhere:

- *In how I spoke up at work*

- In the risks I took creatively

- In the boundaries I started setting

- In the conversations I once avoided

- In the projects I launched without knowing exactly how

And I can trace it all back to one decision:
Saying yes to something I felt unqualified for — and doing it anyway.

Because once you stop waiting for permission...
You become dangerous — in the best way possible.
You realize the only difference between you and the people you admire is that they just started.

 Chapter 7 Summary

In this chapter, the author uncovers one of the most powerful and liberating lessons from network marketing: you don't need permission to start. Many of us grow up believing we have to wait to be chosen — to be invited, certified, qualified, or given authority. The author once believed success was reserved for those who had the right credentials or backgrounds.

But network marketing disrupted that belief by offering immediate access to action. No gatekeepers. No interviews. No one is stopping you. It gave the author the audacity to move forward without waiting for anyone else's approval.

The breakthrough came when they realized that leadership, growth, and success all start by stepping in before you feel ready. It's not about being perfect — it's about deciding you're enough to begin. This mindset shift — from waiting to initiating — has rippled through every area of the author's life, unlocking courage, creativity, boundaries, and boldness.

The real lesson? You don't need to be chosen. You just need to choose yourself.

🖊 Reflection Prompts:

- *Where in your life are you still waiting for someone else's permission?*

- *What's something you've been telling yourself you're not "qualified" to do yet?*

- *When have you held back because you thought you needed more experience, education, or validation?*

- *What would you start today if you believed you were already enough?*

- *How can you start showing up as the person you're becoming — right now?*

Workbook Section:

Exercise 1: Waiting List Inventory

Write down the areas where you've been waiting for someone else to approve, validate, or invite you.

Example:

- *Posting content*
- *Applying for leadership roles*
- *Starting a creative project*
- *Speaking up in meetings*

Now, cross out the "waiting" and write your own permission slip next to each.

<u>PERMISSION SLIP</u>
I hereby give MYSELF permission to:

                    Signed:..
                                    The Authoritative Party

Example:
Posting content → I post now because my voice matters.
Applying for leadership → I lead now because I can grow into it.
Starting a creative project → I begin now because I don't need to be perfect to start.

Exercise 2: Audacity Action Plan

Pick one area from your list where you will stop waiting.

Write:

I am choosing to start:

_____

My first brave step will be:

_____

I will take this step by (date):

_____

Example:
I am choosing to start sharing weekly video tips. My first brave step will be recording my first video this Saturday. I will post it by Sunday.

Exercise 3: Courageous Self-Talk

When you hear yourself thinking:

- *"Who am I to do this?"*
- *"I'm not ready."*
- *"What if people don't take me seriously?"*

Reframe it using:

- *"Why not me?"*
- *"Everyone starts somewhere."*
- *"What's the worst that happens? I grow."*

Write your new go-to self-affirmation:

I don't need to be chosen. I choose myself. I lead. I act. I grow.

◎ Key Takeaway:

The people you admire aren't special because they were chosen. They're special because they started.

📖 Chapter 8: It Was Never About the Company

When I started, I thought the company was the answer. It had the best product. The best training. The best team culture.
The "perfect" opportunity to build a better life.

And for a while, I believed it. I needed to believe it.
Because when you're in deep—spending time, energy, and belief—you have to think you're building something that matters. Something solid. Something lasting.

But as time went on, cracks began to show.
Not just in the company...
But in me.

I started asking questions I hadn't asked before:
If this product disappeared tomorrow... what would I actually have?

If I left this company... would my relationships still stand?

Who am I without the mission statement someone else gave me?

And the answer was uncomfortable at first.
Because I realized I had mistaken community for true belonging.
I had mixed up purpose with product.
And I had held on, thinking loyalty was growth—even when the fit wasn't right anymore.

Leaving Without Bitterness

Let me be clear: this isn't a takedown chapter.
I'm not here to bash a company or point fingers.
Because truthfully, I'm grateful for what I gained:

- The people skills

- The confidence

- The resilience

- The leadership lessons

- The exposure to big thinking

- The personal growth that was, at times, brutal but beautiful

But I can be grateful and honest.
And the honest truth is:
The company was just the container. The growth was mine.

Once I saw that, I stopped clinging out of obligation.
I stopped measuring my worth by ranks, sales, or team size.
I stopped believing that leaving meant failing.

Because what I had built—internally—couldn't be taken away.
I left the company.
But I didn't leave the lessons.

Redefining Success on My Terms

For a long time, success had a very specific shape:

- A certain rank

- A team that duplicated

- A dream board life

- Stage recognition

- Weekly calls and "momentum"

But leaving helped me redefine it.

Now, success means:

- Living in alignment

- Creating without fear

- Showing up honestly

- Doing work that lights me up

- Building something my way—even if it's slower, messier, or doesn't look "shiny" from the outside

And here's the irony:
Once I let go of chasing success inside the system, I started feeling successful in real life.
I became clearer.
More grounded.
More creative.
More courageous.

Because I was no longer trying to force my future to fit inside someone else's blueprint.

The Company Was Just the Start

I thought I was joining a business.
But what I really joined... was a mirror.

It showed me where I people-pleased.
Where I avoided discomfort.
Where I confused worth with validation.
Where I waited for permission.

It revealed my blind spots and strengths.
It woke me up.
And then... it let me go.

And honestly? That was the greatest gift.

Chapter 8 Summary:

In this chapter, we explore the profound realization that personal growth isn't tied to a company, a product, or a specific opportunity—it comes from within. The author reflects on the journey from attaching identity to an organisation to discovering that the true value was never in the company itself, but in the internal transformation that occurred along the way. Through honest self-questioning, they uncover the difference between community and true belonging, purpose and product, loyalty and personal alignment. Leaving the company was not a failure—it was a stepping stone to building a life and success on their own terms. This chapter encourages readers to examine what they've been tethered to and to courageously redefine success in their own lives.

✎ Reflection Prompts:

- Have you ever attached your identity to a job, company, or external label? How did that shape your self-worth?

- If the organisation or role you're currently invested in disappeared tomorrow, what would remain? What would you take with you?

- What is your current definition of success? Where did that definition come from?

- Are there places in your life where you are confusing community with belonging or loyalty with growth?

- What parts of your growth journey do you truly own, regardless of where you gained them?

Workbook Section:

Exercise 1: Unpacking Identity

Write down all the labels, roles, or affiliations you currently use to describe yourself (e.g., job title, company, relationship status, memberships).

Now ask yourself:

- If I lost this label tomorrow, would I still know who I am?

- What parts of me exist without needing external validation?

Exercise 2: Redefining Success

Old Definition of Success:

- What did success used to mean to me?

- Where did this definition come from? (Family, company culture, society?)

New Definition of Success:

- What does success look and feel like for me now?

- How can I align my daily actions with this new definition?

Exercise 3: Lessons You Keep

List 3–5 key skills, mindsets, or lessons you've gained from previous roles, companies, or organisations.
 Next to each one, write how you can apply that lesson in your life today, independent of where you originally learned it.

Skill, Mindset or Lesson	Application to Life today

◎ Key Takeaway:

The company was never the source of your worth—it was simply the environment that helped reveal your strength. True success comes when you build your life on your own terms, not someone else's blueprint.

📖 Chapter 9: The Real Win — Who You Become

I joined for the money. Let's be honest — most of us do.
I saw the lifestyle, the freedom, the passive income.
I wanted the time flexibility, the recognition, the "be your own boss" life.

I joined hoping for more.
More income.
More confidence.
More opportunities.

And I did get more — just not in the way I expected.

Because I didn't walk away with a six-figure team.
I didn't walk away with trophies, titles, or the dream car.

What I walked away with was something harder to measure but impossible to fake:
I became someone I actually respect.

The Gap Between Who You Are and Who You Pretend to Be

In the early days of network marketing, I was performing.
Saying the right things.
Posting the right quotes.

Trying to look like a leader even when I felt completely lost.

I was chasing a version of success I saw around me — not realizing it was more costume than character.

But something wild happened when things didn't go to plan.
When the dream didn't materialize like it was "supposed to."
When I hit my limit.

The mask slipped, and underneath, I found someone real.
Someone resilient.
Someone resourceful.
Someone done pretending.

That version of me didn't need ranks or applause — just alignment.

I Didn't Win in the Way They Measured It

No, I didn't build a legacy team.
No, I didn't max out the comp plan.
No, I didn't become the "overnight success story."

But here's what I did do:
I showed up when it was uncomfortable.
I kept promises to myself when no one was watching.

I built discipline, courage, communication, and confidence.
I found my voice.
I left when it was no longer true.

And let me tell you: that's winning.

Because most people stay in places they've outgrown out of fear or pride.
I didn't.
I chose integrity.
I chose growth.
I chose me.

You Don't Always Get What You Came For...

...but sometimes you get something better.

Network marketing was never the end goal.
It was a tough, no-nonsense training ground.
It was the first time I dared to believe I could build something bigger than a job title.
The first time I invested in my growth.
The first time I said yes before I felt ready — and let the process make me ready.

And even though the chapter ended... the story didn't.

Because I walked away with:
A stronger mindset

Better people skills
Clearer values and vision
A better relationship with failure
And an unshakeable belief that I can figure things out

That's what no rank can ever measure:
Who you become when no one is cheering.

Chapter 9 Summary:

This chapter reveals a powerful truth: sometimes the prize isn't what you came for — it's who you become along the way. Initially driven by the promise of money, lifestyle, and freedom, the author entered network marketing chasing external success. But as the journey unfolded, it became clear that the real reward wasn't a rank, a title, or a dream car — it was an internal transformation.

Through struggle, disappointment, and learning to let go of performative success, the author discovered resilience, discipline, authenticity, and self-respect. This chapter invites readers to stop measuring success by what the world can see and start honouring the quiet victories of showing up, staying true to yourself, and choosing growth over comfort.

✏️ Reflection Prompts:

- What was your original motivation for starting your current journey? Has your "why" evolved?

- Are there areas of your life where you're still wearing a mask or chasing someone else's version of success?

- When have you chosen integrity over comfort? What did that decision teach you?

- How do you measure success today? Are those measures aligned with your true values?

- What qualities or skills have you developed that no one else can see, but you know are life-changing?

Workbook Section:

Exercise 1: Honest Motivations

Write down why you first started your current venture, job, or goal.

Now ask yourself:

- Does this still light me up?

- If not, what motivates me now?

Exercise 2: The Quiet Wins

List 3–5 moments in your life where you made the harder choice — the one aligned with your integrity, even when no one else noticed or cheered.

Moment	Write about why those moments matter to you now.

Exercise 3: Becoming vs. Achieving

Create two columns:

- In Column 1, list achievements or goals you've chased that were externally focused (titles, income, recognition).

- In Column 2, list the skills, mindsets, or character traits you've developed along the way.

External achievements	Internal achievements

Compare the two lists:

- Which list feels more meaningful today?

- How can you consciously invest in the "becoming" side moving forward?

◎ Key Takeaway:

The greatest win is not the title you earn but the person you become when no one is watching.

📖 Chapter 10: How It All Shows Up Now

What happens after you close a chapter in life? Do you really leave it all behind?

When I left network marketing, I didn't walk away empty-handed. I took something far more valuable than titles, ranks, or recognition.

I took myself.

I took the lessons I learned in the trenches: confidence, discipline, courage, and leadership — not just as concepts, but as parts of who I had become.

The Transformation You Can't See

In those early days, I was chasing external wins — numbers, status, applause. But what stuck with me was internal. The resilience to keep going. The discipline to show up even when it was uncomfortable. The courage to speak my truth and set boundaries.

I moved from fearing confrontation and chasing approval to navigating hard talks with honesty and empathy. I learned to value integrity over popularity. And every day, I use the tools I sharpened in the trenches: clear communication, accountability, self-respect.

The Company Was Never the Point

The company was just the stage — but the real story was the growth that happened behind the scenes. It showed me where I people-pleased, where I avoided discomfort, where I outsourced my confidence. And it gave me the space to rewrite those patterns.

Leaving didn't mean losing. It meant graduating.

You Didn't Fail. You Graduated.

Most people stay stuck out of fear — fear of failure, fear of judgment, fear of the unknown. I didn't. I chose growth. I chose integrity. I chose to honor the person I was becoming, not just the goals I had set.

Who you became — that's the win you carry with you forever.

How It Shows Up Now

The skills, mindset, and strength I developed didn't disappear. They show up every day:

- *In how I lead my own life now, with intention and honesty.*

- In the creative risks I take without waiting for permission.

- In the boundaries I set that protect my energy and values.

- In the confidence to say no, to pivot, and to keep moving forward.

This journey taught me that true success isn't about reaching a destination — it's about the growth you embody along the way.

Chapter 10 Summary:

This chapter explores the lasting transformation that happens when you close one chapter and step into the next. The author reflects on leaving network marketing not as an end, but as a graduation — carrying forward invaluable skills like discipline, courage, and leadership. The company was merely the backdrop for a deeper internal journey, revealing patterns and catalyzing growth. Success is redefined as who you become, not what you achieve externally. Readers are invited to honor their own ongoing evolution and recognize that the real wins show up in unexpected, everyday ways.

🖊 *Reflection Prompts:*

- *What lessons from past chapters of your life are still shaping who you are today?*

- *Where have you seen growth in yourself that no one else notices but you?*

- *How can you embrace your own "graduation" moments — leaving behind what no longer serves you and stepping into something new?*

- *In what ways do your daily choices reflect the person you want to become?*

- *What tools or mindsets from your past experiences can you use to navigate your current challenges?*

Workbook Section:

Exercise 1: Growth Inventory

List 3–5 qualities, skills, or mindsets you developed during a past challenge or chapter in your life.
Next to each, write how it shows up in your life now.

Challenge induced Quality, Skills or Mindset	How it shows up

Exercise 2: Graduation Reflection

Think about a time you "graduated" from a role, job, or situation.
  Write about:

- *What you left behind.*

- *What you took with you.*

- *How it shaped the next step.*

Exercise 3: Daily Growth Actions

Identify & write down 2 small daily habits that help you embody your growth and values.

1.

2.

Examples:

- *Practicing honest self-talk.*
- *Setting clear boundaries.*
- *Taking a creative risk.*

Track your progress over the next week and reflect on the impact.

◎ Key Takeaway:

You don't fail when you leave — you graduate. The real win isn't what you achieve; it's who you become along the way. And that growth shows up every day in how you live, lead, and love.

✨ Epilogue: For the Ones Still in It

I see you.

You're in the thick of it — still chasing the vision. Still holding the dream. Still navigating the doubt, the awkward conversations, the late-night content, the pep talks no one else hears.

You're posting with shaking hands.
 You're joining calls while making dinner.
 You're wrestling with the numbers that don't add up.
 You're trying to sound confident when you don't quite believe it yet.

You're exhausted.
 You're proud.
 You're frustrated.
 You're hopeful.

You're in the *messy middle* — that uncertain, stretch-too-thin space where everything feels like effort and nothing feels like evidence.

And still… you show up.

That matters more than you think.

I didn't write this book from the top of the mountain.
I wrote it from the trails.
The seasons.
The pivots.
The in-between.

I wrote it because maybe — just maybe — you're somewhere in the middle too.

And I want you to know this:

You're not failing because it's hard.
You're not behind because it's taking time.
You're not broken because you still doubt yourself.

You're human.

I don't know if you'll stay in the business.
I don't know if it'll be the thing that changes your life.
I don't know where this road leads for you.

But I hope you never confuse your *outcome* with your *worth*.
You are valuable — now.
You are capable — now.
You are allowed to believe in something bigger than what currently exists.

It's easy to laugh at people who dream big.
But it's harder — braver — to *be* one of them.

Maybe you're chasing a version of your life you can't yet see, but deeply feel.
Maybe you're learning how to lead, even as your voice shakes.
Maybe you've already outgrown the version of you who once needed permission to begin.

That matters. That counts.

You're not just building a business.
You're building *you*.

So whether you stay, evolve, pivot, pause, leap, or let go…

Know this:

You never needed a company to validate your worth.
 You always had permission — you just needed to believe it.

And now?

Maybe you do.

You do.

> **"Not all victories are loud. Some are just the quiet decisions to keep going."**

📚 Recommended Reading List

For Your Growth, Confidence, and Courage

These books have inspired not only me, but thousands of others to think differently, act boldly, and cultivate the mindset needed to create lasting success—in business and in life.

Whether you're looking to sharpen your communication skills, reset your financial future, or step into your personal power, you'll find something here to support you at every stage of the journey.

And if reading isn't your thing? No worries—most of these titles are also available in audio format.

---

1. *Skills with People* by Les Giblin

This was the book that changed everything for me; simply 44 pages of gold. It is a timeless classic and is a crash course in human connection. Giblin breaks down the psychology of effective communication with practical strategies for building rapport, resolving conflict, and making people feel seen and heard. A must-read for anyone in leadership, sales, or customer relationships.

2. *Rich Dad Poor Dad* by Robert T. Kiyosaki

Part memoir, part financial manifesto — this book turns traditional thinking on money and employment upside down. Kiyosaki contrasts the financial beliefs of his "rich dad" and "poor dad," encouraging readers to break out of the 9–5 mindset and build assets that generate true wealth.

3. *Cashflow Quadrant* by Robert T. Kiyosaki

A deeper dive into financial independence, this book introduces the four types of income earners: Employee, Self-Employed, Business Owner, and Investor. It challenges you to shift your mindset and move toward greater freedom through leverage and investment.

4. *The 7 Habits of Highly Effective People* by Stephen R. Covey

A foundational personal development book that teaches how to live with intention, integrity, and impact. Covey's principles help readers move from reactive to proactive living, and the habits outlined here are essential for anyone building a values-driven life or business.

5. *There's a Lipstick in My Briefcase* by Karen Salmansohn

Karen is not only an amazing entrepreneur but a brilliant speaker with a truly inspirations story. This book is unny, fierce, and relatable — this book empowers women to show up confidently in their careers without compromising femininity or integrity. It's a great read for anyone navigating leadership, ambition, and self-worth in the business world.

6. *Start with Why* by Simon Sinek

If you haven't heard of Simon Sinek... What rock have you been under?

A quick Google search will lead you to a wealth of wisdom about emotional intelligence, ethical leadership, and purposeful living. *Start with Why* explores how great leaders and organisations inspire action—not by pushing what they do, but by deeply connecting to **why** they do it.

If you've ever struggled with motivation, purpose, or alignment, this book will change the way you show up.

It's a must-read for anyone building a purpose-driven brand, team, or life.

P.S. Another one of his books, *Leaders Eat Last*, is still on my wish list — and honestly, Simon Sinek would be top of my dream dinner guest list. I'd love to have a meal and a conversation with someone who leads with so much heart and clarity.

---

7. *The Big Leap* by Gay Hendricks

This transformational book helps you identify and break through your "Upper Limit Problem" — the self-sabotage that keeps you from living fully in your zone of genius. Essential for anyone who's ready to stop settling and start soaring.

---

8. *Atomic Habits* by James Clear

A practical guide to making small, powerful changes that stick. Clear explains how habits are built (and broken) and gives easy-to-follow strategies for stacking good habits and eliminating the ones that hold you back. Ideal for readers seeking consistency and progress.

---

9. *Everything is Figureoutable* by Marie Forleo

Part pep talk, part toolkit, this book is for the go-getters who feel stuck or scared. Forleo's mantra — "everything is figureoutable" — is more than catchy; it's a mindset that unlocks creativity, resilience, and resourcefulness.

---

10. *The Confidence Code* by Katty Kay & Claire Shipman

A deep look at what confidence really is, how it's formed, and why it matters — especially for women. Drawing on research, interviews, and personal stories, the authors deliver powerful takeaways for anyone who's ever doubted their worth.

---

11. *You Are a Badass* by Jen Sincero

This straight-talking, no-fluff guide to self-belief and mindset is equal parts spiritual and sassy. Sincero helps readers break past fear and excuses to create the life (and income) they truly want. A fun and empowering read.

www.ingramcontent.com/pod-product-compliance
Lightning Source LLC
Chambersburg PA
CBHW020542080526
44583CB00013B/954